3 INGREDIENTS OR SO...

easy, healthy, everyday cooking

TAMILA URAZAYEVA

3 INGREDIENTS OR SO…
Easy, Healthy, Everyday Cooking
Copyright ©2019 by Tamila Urazayeva

The content of this book is for general informational purposes only. It is not meant to be used, nor should it be used, to diagnose or treat any medical condition or to replace the services of your physician or other healthcare provider. The advice and strategies contained in the book may not be suitable for all readers. Please consult your healthcare provider for any questions that you may have about your own medical situation. Neither the author, publisher, nor any of their employees or representatives guarantees the accuracy of information in this book or its usefulness to a particular reader, nor are they responsible for any damage or negative consequence that may result from any treatment, action taken, or inaction by any person reading or following the information in this book

Published by EasyStepsWellness

ISBN-13: 978-1-7336453-0-0
SBN-10: 1-7336453-0-6

Printed in the United States of America

Editor: Alison Hall

Design: Amie Olson

Photography: Poopak Mahdavi

Lenara Batalova

Maya Baghirova

Illustration: AlmatyKitap

Index: Judy Gordon

To my boys—Sergey, Daniel, and Andrew
You are my Everything

To my parents—For your unconditional love
and support in everything I do

CONTENTS

INTRODUCTION

With the recent explosion in popularity of healthy eating and wellness, everyone seems to be talking about new food theories and diets, new ingredients and super-foods. But for many people, figuring out how to bring a focus on health and wellness to their busy lives can be complicated and confusing.

How many times have you found yourself wanting to try a beautiful new recipe until you saw the long list of fancy ingredients you didn't recognize, did not have in your kitchen, or couldn't locate at a local grocery store? It has happened to me—and still does! However, I strongly believe that making good food does not have to be complicated. Healthy meals can come from basic ingredients that you probably have in your kitchen already.

I often hear clients and friends say, "I will not make this dish because it sounds too complicated." But if I say it takes only three ingredients to make healthy dark chocolate at home, it gets attention! Most people are willing to try a three-ingredient recipe that makes a healthy and wholesome dish.

Let me be honest upfront and tell you that some recipes in this book actually do require no more than three ingredients to make. However, others require three "or so" (that is, more than three). My goal is simply to get you trying to make some rather simple dishes that could be very healthy for you.

Most of the recipes in this book are on the healthier side, but I have also included my Pavlova, with its fine white sugar, and, yes, heavy whipping cream. It is so worth it, just this once! This is my philosophy: It is all about the balance. I never did well with diets or any sort of food deprivation for extended periods of time. Instead, I stick to moderation in everything I eat, and I have a little of pretty much everything I like—while choosing healthier and higher-quality options, of course. Healthy eating is about making smart choices. When you make those choices consistently, your taste buds change and you end up craving what's good for your body and mind.

I never believed in "science eating" or counting calories. I find it confusing and deceiving, as foods with the same number of calories can offer a very different nutritional content. For me, eating is about quality over quantity, enjoying every bite

I take, and fueling my body with the right nutrients to have enough energy for a high-performance life. Having a busy schedule, being a mom, traveling around the world, running my business, and working in a corporate environment pushed me to find easier yet more deliciously nutritious ways to cook at home.

Here, I want to share what I've learned with you. This book will give you the lowdown on healthy cooking staples as well as my personal favorite ingredients and kitchen tools that will make your cooking experience easier and healthier.

While I did take culinary classes, my best training came in the kitchen with my mom. Early on, she taught me that the food you eat affects the way you feel and look, whether it's the complexion and texture of your skin, puffy eyes, headaches, poor sleep, or a bloated stomach. All of these (and more) could well be related to your diet. Eating the right foods also can help you limit the need to use conventional medicines. That's another lesson I learned from my mom, who completed years of professional medical training, taught medical school students herself, and yet strongly believes that food can be powerful medicine.

Obviously I have not eaten right and healthy every single day of my life for the last 40+ years! I remember craving white chocolate and sweets in the afternoon in my early 20s, when I started my career in financial services. It seemed to be the norm, just like starting the day with coffee. None of this affected me much back then, just some energy dips throughout the day.

It was when I became pregnant with my first son that I started to really research nutrition and pay close attention to the quality of the ingredients that went into my food. I wanted to give only the best to the growing life inside. Luckily, we lived close to a farmer's market and this reinforced my desire to cook with the freshest possible ingredients. I had never heard the term "organic" prior to moving to the United States. But when I learned that "organic" meant minimal pesticides and chemicals, this became my main choice for everything.

I returned to work a few years after my older son was born. I was again in the fast-paced, fast food, quick lunch, takeout environment. During busy seasons, I would sometimes resort to "office food," and that's when I really could feel the difference between eating quality meals and eating convenience food. At that point, I knew I had to master a quick and easy healthy cooking craft of my own. It was no longer just me and my wellbeing at stake—I had a growing family to nourish daily. While I never got into a meal prep routine, I did get smarter about grocery shopping, buying basic ingredients that I could easily use for different meals throughout the week.

Over the years I have adapted many of the recipes I grew up on so that I could make them from readily available ingredients and make them healthier, more nutritious, and kid-friendly too. I went to a nutrition school to formalize my knowledge and, best of all, to learn how to navigate the growing world of health and wellness with ease and tranquility. I am careful with new food theories and fad diets. Instead, I listen to my body and what it really needs and make small tweaks and adjustments as I go. Everybody is different and knowing how to nourish yourself in order to have more energy, a clearer mind, and better sleep is critical.

Granted, it is not only about the food on your plate. There are many other factors at play in your overall health. Your sleep, physical activity, and social life also contribute to your emotional, mental, and physical health. But in my opinion food is a great start and one of those easier to control and manage aspects of your life. Most important, providing your body with the food it needs and loves is a highly enjoyable and delicious experience!

I invite you into my kitchen, as all of the recipes in this book
are dishes I have loved and been cooking for years—
now they are yours to enjoy too.

INGREDIENTS

Having high-quality ingredients on hand is an essential step in healthy cooking and eating. I personally do not like to cook something that calls for a "special order" ingredient that you might use only once. That being said, I might introduce you to some ingredients you do not have in your kitchen just yet. Usually these are basic ingredients—staples in modern, healthy cooking that would be well worth investing in. While these healthy cooking staples can be used in many different recipes, keep in mind that in most cases you can use substitutions as well.

I strongly believe in quality. In a nutshell, you cannot make a healthy and high-quality dish without high-quality ingredients. I always go with quality rather than quantity in my pantry, and it is generally a win-win.

MY GO-TO INGREDIENTS

DRY GOODS

Organic brown rice noodles
Organic wheat pasta
Organic all-purpose flour
Baking soda

Gluten-free flours

Almond flour or meal
Coconut flour
Buckwheat flour
Cassava flour

Grains, seeds, and nuts

Nuts and seeds
Quinoa
Oats (gluten-free)
Buckwheat
Millet

OILS/FATS

Coconut oil
Olive oil
Avocado oil
Ghee

VINEGARS

Apple cider vinegar
Balsamic vinegar

CANNED GOODS

Coconut milk
Chickpeas

FRIDGE

Pasture-raised eggs
Grass-fed butter

SPICES/CONDIMENTS/SAUCES

Himalayan pink salt
Celtic sea salt
Black pepper
Dried thyme
Dried rosemary
Tahini
Dijon mustard

SWEETENERS

Dried fruits
Raw honey
Maple syrup
Bananas

PRODUCE

Onions
Garlic
Carrots
Lemons
Avocados
Fresh herbs
Fresh leafy greens
Celery
Cucumbers
Tomatoes
Fresh fruits
Fresh berries

FREEZER

Berries and other fruit
Organic chicken
Organic grass-fed beef
Wild fish

COCONUT OIL

This is my go-to fat for baking. However, if you don't mind the sweet flavor, it is also great for sautéing and stir-frying. In all honesty, it's the most versatile oil in my house, as I use it outside kitchen quite a bit too—for moisturizing skin, hair masks, and oil pulling.

OLIVE OIL

Truly liquid gold in my kitchen. I like to just sip it on its own. Adding it to most of my dishes as a finishing touch always seems to elevate the taste and flavors. Make sure you get the freshest, highest-quality extra-virgin olive oil possible, in a dark glass bottle, and consume it within one month of opening.

AVOCADO OIL

If you prefer a neutral taste, then this is your go-to oil for everyday cooking. Not only does avocado oil offer a plethora of health benefits, it also has a high smoke point, which makes it ideal for cooking at higher temperatures, up to 400 degrees F.

GHEE OR CLARIFIED BUTTER

These forms of butter are free of liquid and milk solids, hence they can be used for dairy-free cooking. Ghee is rich in fat-soluble vitamins and is ideal for high-temperature cooking as well. I prefer to make sure it is made from grass-fed butter or at least organic.

VINEGARS

Apple cider vinegar is a great alternative to balsamic vinegar and also can be a substitute for lemon or lime juice. It is rich in probiotics and enzymes. Adding it to your drinking water is alkalinizing and very beneficial for the digestive system. I sometimes use it when baking with baking soda to make the dough light and airy and get rid of the baking soda taste.

SALT

My main condiment. It really does bring up the taste and the flavor of the ingredients in a dish. If using the proper salt, you also get minerals into your diet. Thus, I prefer using high-quality salts, such as Himalayan pink and Celtic sea salt.

TAHINI

This condiment is made by grinding sesame seeds, which unlocks all the benefits these wonder seeds have to offer. Rich in essential nutrients, these ancient seeds help with blood pressure, hormonal balance, nutrient absorption, and more. Tahini is a key ingredient in hummus, but it can also be enjoyed on its own with crudités, in salads and salad dressings, or on toast with a bit of honey. You will find that its taste is more savory than that of most nut and seed butters.

GLUTEN-FREE FLOURS

Even though I do not maintain a 100% gluten-free diet, I have noticed that limiting gluten has major benefits for me. When I use regular wheat (all-purpose) flour I stick to organic, non-GMO options. My favorite gluten-free varieties are almond, coconut, cassava, and buckwheat flour. (Note that even though there is "wheat" in the name, buckwheat flour is gluten-free, as is the grain itself.) These flours are easy to find at any health food store or online—and are also showing up in regular grocery stores as well.

GLUTEN-FREE PASTA

There are many gluten-free options when it comes to pasta, but keep in mind that "gluten-free" does not necessarily equal "healthy." Always check the ingredients! I find that brown rice pasta has a similar taste and texture to regular pasta, as does quinoa pasta. Lentil pasta has a stronger flavor. Thus, I always keep a box or two of brown rice pasta in case I need to make a quick meal, like my easy recipe on page 86.

CHIA SEEDS

This superfood can be pretty essential for a healthy diet as it is a powerhouse of nutrients. Rich in fiber, protein, manganese, omega-3s, and plenty of antioxidants, chia seeds are a great alternative to eggs when it comes to binding and thickening for baking.

NUTS AND SEEDS

All varieties of nuts and seeds are superfoods packed with protein, fiber, vitamins, minerals, and healthy fats. I talk more about the goodness of nuts and how to make the most of their beneficial properties in my "Easy Basics" chapter. Each nut and seed is unique and provides a particular nutrient profile. One important note: Store nuts and seeds in airtight containers and be sure to consume them before they go rancid. Always buy them raw and unsalted, as commercial roasters often damage delicate fats using high roasting temperatures, while also adding unhealthy oils and preservatives.

DRIED FRUITS

These are my go-to natural sweeteners. Dried figs, dates, raisins, apricots, goji berries, and mulberries are my personal favorites, with a higher priority given to the last two, as they are lowest on the glycemic index. These are true superfoods, rich in antioxidants, phytonutrients, vitamins, and minerals. They're high in natural sugars, too, so consume them in moderation.

HONEY

Raw honey is much more than a natural sweetener; it has been used as medicine for centuries. Raw honey contains amino acids, minerals, vitamins, and enzymes. The key is to buy high-quality raw honey, preferably in a glass container. There are many highly processed varieties on the market and the best option is to buy local honey from a beekeeper that you know. Even though raw honey never goes bad and does not need any special storage or refrigeration, I keep mine in a glass jar with a lid on and away from heat and direct sunlight.

QUINOA

This ancient seed has gained huge popularity lately. Gluten-free and a complete protein source, quinoa is loaded with vitamins, minerals, fiber, and antioxidants, helps with blood sugar regulation, and has anti-inflammatory properties as well. It is very quick to make, and while I personally prefer it as a savory ingredient, it can also be used as a breakfast option topped with sweet dried fruits and nut milk.

OATS

This grain is naturally gluten-free; however, due to possible cross-contamination, you have to look for "gluten-free" on the label if you are concerned about gluten. There is so much goodness in oats as they contain high amounts of protein, fiber, all of the B vitamins, manganese, selenium, magnesium, and so on. They help to keep you satiated for longer, providing major benefits for your heart health. I strongly recommend that you seek organic, gluten-free varieties. You can make easy overnight oats that will be ready in the morning for a nutritious breakfast (page 34), or cooked oatmeal topped with superfoods (page 37), or my delicious oatmeal cookies (page 114).

BUCKWHEAT

This is another ancient grain that is a complete protein source with a long list of health benefits. (Note that even though "wheat" is in the name, buckwheat is gluten-free.) This superfood is packed with antioxidants, fiber, vitamins, and minerals. In addition, it helps with heart health by lowering cholesterol and blood-sugar levels, and it has anti-inflammatory properties too. Buckwheat works incredibly well as a substitute for rice in many dishes. I love it for breakfast, topped with a few superfoods and a splash of nut milk. I have noticed that it keeps me feeling full longer and it's also a benefit to my skin, as it contains high amounts of iron and magnesium.

MILLET

My other "beauty grain," millet is actually an ancient, gluten-free seed. It is easily digestible, high in fiber, vitamins, and minerals, and low on the glycemic index. It is absolutely delicious and can be used in many different recipes. You can make it with a creamy consistency or fluffy like quinoa or rice. I try to have millet in the morning at least once a week.

FRESH FRUITS AND VEGETABLES

The first rule of a healthy diet is to eat fresh fruits and vegetables daily! You have heard the expression "Eat the rainbow" and that's what I strive for every single day. Different phytonutrients are responsible for the various colors in fresh produce and also provide the body with all sorts of powerful nutrients that protect us from diseases, fight against free radicals, and provide us with a variety of vitamins, minerals, fiber, proteins, and fats. I stock up on fresh produce once or twice a week and always have a few staples on hand such as lemons, carrots, onions, garlic, and avocados, along with some fresh greens and herbs for salads, green juices, and smoothies. Each week I usually buy some fresh berries, apples, bananas, and other in-season produce. And just in case, I always have some frozen berries and other fruits in the freezer too, as they are ideal for smoothies or a cold sweet treat.

GROCERY STORE TERMINOLOGY

When it comes to produce shopping, the most common question I hear is, "Should I buy organic or conventional?"

My answer is simple: Organic, as much as it is practically possible. Organic fruits and vegetables taste better, have higher amounts of vitamins and minerals, and limit your exposure to pesticides and toxins that result from conventional farming. On the down side, organic is not always available and it is generally more expensive.

The good news is that not all fruits and vegetables attract critters and absorb the same amount of chemicals from conventional farming. So there are instances where buying organic produce may not be as critical. Every year, the Environmental Working Group (EWG) releases two lists—the Clean Fifteen and the Dirty Dozen—that health-conscious shoppers can use as up-to-date guidance for when buying organic is a must and when buying nonorganic is OK.

DIRTY DOZEN

Always buy organic

 STRAWBERRIES

 SPINACH

 NECTARINES

 APPLES

 GRAPES

 PEACHES

 CHERRIES

 PEARS

 TOMATOES

 CELERY

 POTATOES

 SWEET BELL PEPPERS

CLEAN FIFTEEN

OK to buy conventional

 AVOCADOS

 SWEET CORN

 PINEAPPLES

 CABBAGE

 ONIONS

 SWEET PEAS, FROZEN

 PAPAYAS

 ASPARAGUS

 MANGOES

 EGGPLANTS

 HONEYDEW MELONS

 KIWIS

 CANTALOUPES

 CAULIFLOWER

 BROCCOLI

LOCAL

Another term to consider is local. What could be better than knowing where your food is coming from, knowing about the soil, the plants, the seeds, and most important, the process involved in growing the food? If you have access to a farm that you trust, this is your best option. When you see the term "local" at your grocery store, it generally means the food was grown within a 150-mile radius. Therefore you know it is in season and fresher than produce imported from afar. If it is local and organic you get the best of both worlds. However, it's generally safe to give priority to organic options for the Dirty Dozen and local for the Clean Fifteen when shopping at a grocery store. Farmer's markets also are an excellent place to find local and organic produce, but always do your research and ask questions about the farmers' processes.

GMO (GENETICALLY MODIFIED ORGANISMS)

I am a firm believer that you are what you eat and without going into details of all the concerns associated with GMO foods, I just avoid them as much as possible. Foods that are most likely to contain GMOs are corn, soybeans, canola, cotton, squash, zucchini, papaya, wheat, peas, sugar beets, and salmon. Unfortunately, this list is not complete, so buying organic is generally your best bet to avoid GMO.

ANIMAL PRODUCTS

I believe it is essential to consume the cleanest and highest-quality animal products available to you. That means grass-fed for beef, pasture-raised for chicken, and wild for fish. Organic is another consideration to limit exposure to antibiotics, growth hormones, and most conventional toxic chemicals.

KITCHEN TOOLS

There are a few essential tools that I must have in my kitchen, and I believe you will find them useful too. Although I resist fancy gadgets that serve a single purpose, I find my spiralizer and my ice-cream maker quite handy and fun, especially when cooking with and for kids.

POTS AND PANS

My all-time favorite brand is Le Creuset, the French cookware. I use the enameled cast-iron 5½-quart round Dutch oven for most of my cooking. It is great for making broths, soups, and stews, as well as for sautéing, roasting, and slow cooking in the oven. The interior is non-reactive, heats up evenly, and is easy to clean. I also use the classic enameled cast-iron 1¾-quart saucepan. A rectangular 9 x 13-inch stoneware baking dish works for most of my oven baking and roasting. However, any other good quality stoneware or glass baking dish will suffice for this purpose.

BLENDER

Having a high-speed blender can save you a lot of time and make your life much easier. My favorite brand is Vitamix, and it is super easy to use and clean. It can do it all from blending soups to making dough, nut butters and milks, sauces, smoothies, and more.

FOOD PROCESSOR

I recommend a small food processor for chopping or grating vegetables, fruits, and fresh herbs. It's great for chopping whole nuts, too.

UNBLEACHED PARCHMENT PAPER

I use unbleached parchment paper to make paper pouches and to line baking sheets. It's also very handy when it comes to rolling out any type of dough—and when the dough is too sticky, I might even roll it between two sheets of parchment paper. I do not favor using aluminum foil in my kitchen; when I occasionally use foil to cover a baking pan, I use parchment paper as a barrier before I cover with aluminum foil.

GLASS STORAGE CONTAINERS

Sealable glass storage containers in a variety of sizes and shapes are ideal for storing food. Overall, glass is a safer storage option than plastic. Furthermore, it is good for hot or cold items, for liquid or dry ingredients. The least-expensive, most versatile glass storage option I have found is Mason jars. Different size Mason jars can be used to store spices, nuts and seeds, grains, leftovers, smoothies, nut milks, and salads to go.

STAND OR HAND MIXER

Electric hand mixers work wonders when you need to make batter, beat up some eggs, or whip up some cream. A stand mixer can free up your hands, while a hand mixer can free up space on your countertop. My choice is an inexpensive stand mixer (under $40), which turns into a hand mixer with a press of a button.

CUTTING BOARDS

I prefer to use wood or eco-friendly cutting boards such as bamboo or dishwasher-safe paper-composite boards by Epicurean. Plastic boards are easy to clean in the dishwasher, but be aware that when they are used for a long time small plastic fibers can come off and make their way into your food. I highly recommend having a separate board for raw meats.

JUICER

A quick way to get a boost of nutrients right into your system is through a freshly squeezed juice. My all-time favorite juicer is the masticating Omega juicer. It takes a bit longer than a centrifugal juicer, but it yields more juice and the juice doesn't oxidize as quickly, meaning you can refrigerate it for up to 48 hours.

SPIRALIZER

This is not an essential tool, but it is so much fun to have. Using the spiralizer is my trick to engage my little one to help in the kitchen and eat veggies too. The spiralizer makes a veggie pasta in minutes, so if you are on a mission to avoid traditional wheat pasta, this will help. Zucchini, squash, carrots, cucumbers, sweet potatoes, or just about any vegetable can be turned into noodle-like strands.

ICE-CREAM MAKER

This is another "extra" kitchen tool that is fun for kids, especially during summer months when I try to keep the cool treats healthy. You do not have to buy a state-of-the-art machine; a very basic one will do the trick.

BREAKFAST

BREAKFAST

MORNING ROUTINE

We all have our morning routines—the simple steps we take to start the day. This routine often sets the tone for the rest of the day, so it is worth putting some thought into it!

One non-negotiable attribute of my mornings, no matter where I am in the world, is drinking water. For me, lukewarm water works best and is less of a shock for my body when I just wake up. I often add some lemon juice or a spoon of apple cider vinegar to my water, as it has an alkalinizing effect on the body, promotes detoxification and weight management, keeps skin glowing, and boosts immunity, energy, and mood, just to name a few benefits! Your body goes through a range of detoxification processes overnight and it is most dehydrated first thing in the morning. Water helps with flushing out the toxins and initial hydration.

I know for sure I cannot skip breakfast! It is amazing how breakfasts often determine what foods I crave throughout the day, whether I end up looking for snacks or have enough energy and stamina for a productive morning. Providing my body with the right nutrients while breaking the night fast is very important to me. All of the breakfast options here have good nutritional profiles and yet are easily prepared with simple, wholesome ingredients.

A NOTE ABOUT HYDRATION

Proper hydration is essential for good health in general and drinking an adequate amount of water throughout the day is critical for all body systems. Follow my 2T2Q rule:

TIMING

Drinking water first thing in the morning and in between meals works best. Drinking water with your meals or right after dilutes the digestive juices and hinders the proper digestion process. Should you need some liquid with your meal, try focusing on better chewing; if that fails, take a few sips of warm tea or water.

TEMPERATURE

Lukewarm or room temperature water does not cause as much stress to the body as ice-cold water. Drinking very warm, almost hot, water is even better as it is soothing for the digestive tract, improves circulation, calms the nervous system, helps with relieving constipation, and aids with overall detoxification.

QUALITY

Investing in a good water filter can be very helpful in ensuring water quality and that you are not ingesting pollutants. It's best to avoid water from plastic bottles and to store water in glass or other non-reactive containers.

QUANTITY

How much water you need to drink is individual, depending upon factors such as diet quality, climate, and physical activity level. A good rough goal is to drink half of your body weight in ounces daily.

3 INGREDIENTS or so...

ALMOND CHIA PUDDING

Don't give up on chia pudding if you don't like it right away. You might try adding some extra toppings to find your perfect combination. Chia pudding is a delicious source of protein, omega-3s, and fiber. This recipe can be made the night before and is great for breakfast, a mid-day snack, or even dessert.

Makes about 1⅓ cups

⅓ cup raw almonds, soaked in ⅔ cup water for at least six hours or overnight, then rinsed well and drained

1 cup filtered water

4 tablespoons chia seeds

1–2 pitted dates *(optional)*

A pinch of salt *(optional)*

Place the soaked and drained almonds along with the filtered water and the optional dates and salt into a blender. Blend for 30–60 seconds until fully pulverized. Pour into a Mason jar and add the chia seeds, mixing very well to prevent clumps from forming.

Leave to thicken for 10–15 minutes, or close the lid on the jar and leave overnight in the fridge. Top with a drizzle of honey, fresh or frozen berries, chopped nuts or seeds, and enjoy.

TIP: *In a pinch you can use pre-made almond milk instead of soaking almonds. Just substitute one cup of almond milk for the almonds and water in this recipe.*

BLUEBERRY CHIA PUDDING

Here is another take on chia pudding. Blueberries add a vitamin boost, a little tartness, and rich, beautiful color. You can try other berries, too. I use cashews to make the milk for this recipe; however, coconut milk or any dairy-free milk of your choice will work as well.

Makes about 1⅓ cups

⅓ cup cashews, soaked in ⅔ cup water for at least two hours, then rinsed well and drained

1 cup filtered water

½ cup fresh or frozen blueberries

4 tablespoons chia seeds

1–2 pitted dates *(optional)*

A pinch of salt *(optional)*

Place the soaked and drained cashews along with the filtered water, blueberries, and optional dates and salt into a blender. Blend for 30–60 seconds until fully pulverized. Pour into a Mason jar and add the chia seeds, mixing very well to prevent clumps from forming.

Leave to thicken for 10–15 minutes, or close the lid on the jar and leave overnight in the fridge. Top with some extra fresh or frozen blueberries and enjoy.

TIP: *In a pinch, instead of soaking for two hours, you can soak the cashews for 10 minutes in hot water, rinse well, and drain. Please note that heat generally destroys enzymes and will reduce the nutritional benefits of cashews.*

3 INGREDIENTS or so...

BANANA BREAD

I often find that bananas go spotty before we can eat them, and this delicious bread is a great way to avoid wasting them. The recipe calls for 2½ cups of almond flour or meal; occasionally I mix 2 cups of almond flour with ½ cup buckwheat flour for extra nutrients and texture.

Makes 1 loaf

4 very ripe bananas

2 medium eggs

4 tablespoons coconut oil

⅓ cup maple syrup

2½ cups almond flour or almond meal

A pinch of salt

A pinch of baking soda

¼ cup walnuts for decoration *(optional)*

Preheat oven to 350 degrees F. Line a loaf pan or small (7 x 4-inch) baking dish with parchment paper.

Using a fork or potato masher, mash the bananas in a bowl, then add the eggs, coconut oil, and maple syrup. Mix well, but it does not have to be perfectly smooth. Add a pinch of baking soda and a pinch of salt, give it another quick mix, then add the almond flour or meal to the banana mash and combine.

Pour the dough into the pan, sprinkle walnuts atop, and bake for 30–40 minutes, depending on the thickness, until the top is golden brown and a toothpick inserted into the center comes out clean. Remove from the oven and let cool for 5–10 minutes before serving.

> TIP: *Another option for brown, spotty bananas is to put them in the freezer to use later in a smoothie, in this banana bread recipe, or for the oatmeal cookie recipe on page 114. None of these recipes specifically calls for frozen bananas, but fresh and frozen work equally well.*

OVERNIGHT OATS

There is nothing better than waking up to a breakfast that's ready for you. Overnight oats are just that! Spend a few minutes at night and you will have a nutritious and delicious breakfast ready in the morning. Most people prefer to eat these oats cold, but if I have an extra moment, I like to heat them up on the stovetop and have a warm porridge. You can make overnight oats with water, while I prefer to use a dairy-free milk for extra creaminess and nutrients.

Serves 1

¾ cup rolled oats (organic and gluten-free preferred)

1 cup almond milk or coconut milk

A pinch of salt

½–1 teaspoon raw honey *(optional)*

1 teaspoon chia seeds *(optional)*

Mix oats, milk, salt, and optional honey and chia seeds in a Mason jar, close the lid tightly, and leave in the fridge overnight (or for at least two hours). Top it off with coconut flakes, chopped nuts or seeds, dried fruits, a spoonful of coconut yogurt, or a little extra milk, if desired.

HOT SUPER GRAINS BREAKFAST

My favorite breakfast option is cooked grains topped with superfoods and a drizzle of fresh olive oil. Don't judge me before you try it. I've been asked if this is a savory or a sweet break-fast—well, it's a mix! You get savory grains with a touch of sweet dried berries. My kids prefer it sweet, so for them I add a teaspoon of honey to the cooked grains. For my breakfast, I may add any or all of the ingredients below, depending on what I have on hand. The toppings add extra nutrition, flavor, texture, and beautiful color. (See page 148 for basic cooking instructions for grains.)

Serves 1

1 cup cooked grains (rolled or steel-cut oats, buckwheat, millet, or quinoa)

½ teaspoon chia seeds

1 teaspoon pumpkin seeds

1 teaspoon sunflower seeds

1 dried fig, thinly sliced

1 teaspoon goji berries

1 teaspoon dried mulberries

1 teaspoon olive oil

Place your favorite grains in a bowl and top with your preferred combination of flavors.

AVOCADO TOAST, TWO WAYS

This is a staple of healthy eating nowadays, partly because it works any time of day—you can enjoy it for breakfast, a snack, even for a light dinner. You may already have your favorite version of avocado toast, but here is what I find works for me. It takes just a few quick minutes to assemble this delicious goodness. Adding a slice of smoked, wild-caught salmon provides an extra protein and omega-3 boost, but I like it mainly for the taste and flavor. I prefer to use sprouted-grain-and-seed bread; however, there are many healthy bread options available, including gluten-free.

Serves 1

1 slice of bread

½ medium ripe avocado

1 slice smoked wild salmon
(*optional*)

A drizzle of olive oil

A pinch of sea salt

Toast a slice of bread and drizzle a bit of olive oil on top. If you want to add salmon, put it on the toast now. Cut an avocado in half. Using the edge of a spoon, scoop out slices of avocado and place them on top of your toast. You may mash the avocado with a fork a bit, although I like to keep the slices intact. Season with a bit of salt and drizzle with additional olive oil.

Other additions you might like: broccoli greens, thin slices of fresh radish, sesame seeds, or dry garlic flakes

SOUPS, SALADS, AND MORE

SOUPS, SALADS, AND MORE

BUTTERNUT SQUASH SOUP

The classic fall staple is pumpkin, of course, but you can use either pumpkin or butternut squash for this soup. The rich orange color of both of these vegetables reveals their massive amounts of vitamin A along with immunity-boosting and inflammation-fighting properties. Butternut squash is also rich in vitamin C and potassium.

Serves 4–6

1 pound butternut squash, peeled and cut into large chunks

1 large yellow onion, chopped

6 cups homemade chicken stock (see my basic stock recipe on page 142)

1 carrot, chopped *(optional)*

2–3 tablespoons olive oil

Salt and pepper

Optional garnishes:

Chopped dill, parsley, or cilantro

Pumpkin seeds

A drizzle of olive oil

In a large, heavy-bottomed stockpot, add the olive oil and onions. Cook over medium heat for 5–7 minutes, until translucent. Add chopped carrot (if using), and sauté for 5 minutes. Add squash, sauté for another 5–7 minutes, and season with salt and pepper.

Cover with chicken stock, bring to a boil, reduce the heat, and simmer for about 20 minutes until the squash and carrot are tender.

Carefully transfer to a blender and blend until smooth and creamy. Transfer the soup back to the pot, season with extra salt and pepper if needed, and serve hot, topped with one or more of the garnishes, if desired.

SUBSTITUTION TIPS: *You can use avocado oil instead of olive oil for sautéing, and vegetable stock (page 145) or water instead of the chicken stock (page 142).*

CHICKEN QUINOA SOUP

A colder-weather favorite! This soup warms you up and provides a bowl full of healthy, comforting nourishment. I prefer to make the broth from scratch, using the chicken meat for the soup.

Serves 6

Chicken stock (See my basic stock recipe on page 142. Two whole chicken legs or a half-chicken will suffice for this soup, yielding 6–8 cups of broth.)

Cooked chicken (from making the stock)

1 medium yellow onion, chopped

1 medium carrot, chopped

2 celery stalks, chopped

1 garlic clove, minced

⅓ cup uncooked quinoa

3–4 tablespoons olive oil

1 small head of broccoli (about ½ pound), cut into florets, stems peeled and diced *(optional)*

½ cup of fresh chopped herbs or scallions *(optional)*

Rinse quinoa and cook with ⅔ cup of water in a small saucepan. (See page 148 for basic cooking instructions for grains.)

In a large Dutch oven over medium heat, add olive oil and onion and sauté for about 5 minutes, while you chop the carrot. Add the chopped carrot and sauté while you chop the celery and dice the broccoli stems. Add celery and broccoli stems to the pan and sauté all the veggies for another 3–5 minutes.

Add the chicken stock and bring to a boil. Meanwhile, chop the cooked chicken meat into bite-sized pieces. Add cooked quinoa, broccoli florets, chicken, and minced garlic to the soup, along with some more salt, if needed. Simmer for another 10–15 minutes until all the veggies are fully cooked. Turn off the heat and let the soup rest for 5–10 minutes. Serve hot with some chopped fresh herbs or scallions.

SOUPS, SALADS, AND MORE

3 INGREDIENTS or so...

BORSCH

Growing up my mom always made borsch with beef and beef-bone broth. Raising my own family, I found that chicken broth is much quicker and easier to make, and that it works for borsch equally well. There is one secret to a good borsch—it always tastes better when it is re-heated the next day. So make plenty, in order to enjoy the leftovers tomorrow.

Serves 6–8

Chicken stock (See my basic chicken broth recipe on page 142. Two whole chicken legs or a half-chicken will suffice for this soup, yielding 6–8 cups of stock.)

Cooked chicken (from making the stock)

1 onion, chopped

1 carrot, julienned

1 medium beet, julienned

½ bell pepper, chopped

1 small tomato, chopped

1 large white potato, chopped into ½-inch cubes

¼ medium-sized head of green cabbage, shredded

2 garlic cloves, minced

3–4 tablespoons olive oil

⅓ cup chopped fresh herbs (dill and/or parsley)

Sour cream for garnish *(optional)*

In a large Dutch oven over medium heat, add the olive oil and onion and sauté for 5–7 minutes; gradually add the carrot, beet, and bell pepper. Continue sautéing for about 10 minutes. Add the tomato and sauté for an additional 3 minutes.

Add the chicken stock and bring to a boil, reduce heat and simmer for 5–10 minutes. Meanwhile, chop the cooked chicken meat into bite-sized pieces. Add the chicken meat, cabbage, and potato to the soup, and continue simmering for 10–15 minutes until the potato and cabbage are tender.

Add the garlic, parsley and/or dill, cover the pot, and turn off the heat. Let the borsch rest for at least 15 minutes. Serve with a tablespoon of sour cream if desired. If you have some borsch left, let it cool completely and store in the refrigerator. When you heat it up the next day, it will have an even richer taste and aroma.

BASIC ROASTED VEGGIES

I love roasting vegetables, as the prep takes almost no time, there are very few ingredients, and the result is always so delicious! For heartier veggies like potatoes, I use only olive oil, salt, pepper, and thyme. For softer veggies like zucchini, I like to add some fresh minced garlic as well. You can always experiment to find your favorite seasoning combinations.

You can mix the veggies together or roast them separately, just be sure to put together those that have about the same cooking time: potatoes (white, purple, and sweet) together with beets, butternut squash, and carrots; and zucchini together with yellow squash, bell peppers, cauli-flower, and broccoli florets. Onions work well in either roasting pan!

3 INGREDIENTS or so...

ROASTED ZUCCHINI AND YELLOW SQUASH

You can roast just the zucchini or just yellow squash, but I like to combine them for extra color.

Serves 4

2 medium zucchini, chopped in half-circles about ⅓-inch wide

2 medium yellow squash, chopped in half-circles about ⅓-inch wide

2 garlic cloves, minced

3–4 tablespoons olive oil

Salt and pepper

Preheat the oven to 450 degrees F.

Pile the zucchini and squash slices in a baking dish or on a baking sheet lined with parchment paper. Add the garlic, drizzle with olive oil, and season with salt and pepper.

Mix together so the veggies are well coated with oil. Spread evenly in the pan. Roast for about 10 minutes, checking periodically. Remove from the oven and toss lightly. Roast for another 5 minutes if needed until the veggies are soft and golden.

ROASTED SWEET POTATOES

Serves 4

2 medium sweet potatoes,
cut into ⅔-inch cubes

2–3 tablespoons olive oil

Salt and pepper

A pinch of dried thyme

Preheat the oven to 450 degrees F.

Placed the sweet potato cubes in a 9 x 13-inch baking dish. Drizzle with the olive oil, generously season with salt, and add pepper and a pinch of thyme. Mix well, making sure the potatoes are fully coated with the oil.

Roast for about 10 minutes, checking periodically. Remove from the oven, toss lightly so they roast evenly on all sides, and return to oven. Roast for another 5–10 minutes or until the potatoes are evenly browned and you can pierce them with a knife.

3 INGREDIENTS or so…

ROASTED GOLDEN POTATOES

Serves 4–6

6 medium golden potatoes,
cut into ⅔-inch cubes

2 tablespoons olive oil

Salt and pepper

A pinch of dried thyme

Preheat the oven to 450 degrees F.

Place the potato cubes in a 9 x 13-inch baking dish, drizzle with olive oil, season generously with salt, and add pepper and a pinch of thyme. Toss the potatoes so they are well coated with oil. Spread evenly in a single layer, but it is fine if you don't make a perfect single layer; you will toss them again later to ensure that they all get evenly browned.

Roast the potatoes for 10–15 minutes. Remove the pan from the oven, give the potatoes a light toss, and roast for another 10 minutes or until they are all golden brown and you can easily pierce them with a knife.

CLASSIC HUMMUS

Hummus is a versatile spread for many occasions. I enjoy it on its own, on a slice of toast, on a cracker, in a salad, or with crudités. When serving to guests, I like to top it with a sprinkle of sesame seeds and a drizzle of olive oil. You can top with paprika and/or finely chopped greens too.

Makes about 2 cups

1 can (15 ounces) organic chickpeas, drained, liquid saved

3 tablespoons of chickpea liquid

2–3 garlic cloves, peeled

⅓ cup tahini

Juice of one lemon (about 6 tablespoons)

1 tablespoon olive oil

1 teaspoon salt

Put all the ingredients in a food processer and pulse until smooth and creamy. It is that easy!

PESTO

Pesto is easy to make and it tastes wonderful when freshly made. I sometimes use parsley instead of, or together with, basil and experiment with different nuts. You can try almonds or cashews instead of pine nuts. There is no excuse to use store-bought pesto when you have the ingredients on hand.

Makes about 1 cup

1 cup fresh basil leaves and stalks

½ cup pine nuts

1 garlic clove, peeled

¼ cup olive oil

Juice of half a lemon (about 3 tablespoons)

A pinch of salt

Put all the ingredients in a food processor and pulse until smooth. Enjoy this pesto with pasta, in salads, with crackers or crudités, or on its own—it's that delicious!

TIP: *Turn the pesto into a creamier, even more nutritious and delicious dip or sauce by adding half an avocado to the processor along with the rest of the ingredients.*

GREEN SALAD

You can never go wrong with a simple green salad, which is so light and versatile. I probably have it every other day with any main dish. For the greens, I usually use a box of organic spring mix. Even though it is pre-washed, I give it a quick rinse and spin dry in a salad spinner.

Serves 4

1 box (5 ounces) organic spring mix, washed and dried

1 cucumber, cut in half lengthwise and thinly sliced

5–6 fresh radishes, cut in half and thinly sliced

¼ cup fresh dill, chopped

Combine all the ingredients and toss them with freshly made olive oil and lemon dressing or vinaigrette dressing (page 153).

3 INGREDIENTS or so...

TOMATO AND BURRATA SALAD

This salad can be served with or without burrata cheese. As long as you are using fully ripened heirloom tomatoes, they will be the star of this dish. I love using different color tomatoes— green, orange, red, or purple-red, because they look so beautiful mixed together on the plate.

Serves 4

3–4 medium heirloom tomatoes, cut into large, bite-sized chunks

2 medium balls fresh burrata cheese, quartered

½ cup fresh basil leaves, torn or cut in half

3 tablespoons olive oil

2–3 teaspoons balsamic vinegar

A pinch of salt and pepper

Place the burrata in the middle of a serving platter. Cut the tomatoes in half first and then in big, bite-sized chunks. If you're using smaller tomatoes, you can leave them in halves or quarters, depending on the size and your preference. Place the tomatoes around the burrata and scatter the basil leaves on top.

Drizzle with olive oil and balsamic vinegar and season with salt and pepper. Or, whisk the olive oil and balsamic vinegar together, as in the dressing from page 153, and drizzle it over the cheese and tomatoes.

CHOPPED SUMMER SALAD

This is a colorful fresh salad that can be made with many different ingredients.
These are my favorites:

Serves 4

1 large cucumber

3 Roma or plum tomatoes

½ yellow bell pepper (any color would work)

¼ cup fresh parsley, chopped

¼ cup fresh dill, chopped

¼ sweet onion *(optional)*

Chop the vegetables into ½-inch cubes. Toss with the herbs and an olive oil and lemon dressing or the vinaigrette from page 153.

3 INGREDIENTS or so...

SAUERKRAUT SALAD

This easy salad is a new idea for dressing up traditional sauerkraut.

Serves 2

2 cups sauerkraut (see page 141)

1 fresh tomato, diced

1 small cucumber, diced

¼ cup finely chopped fresh herbs: cilantro and/or parsley and/or dill

1 tablespoon olive oil

Salt and pepper

If your sauerkraut is not salty, season with salt first and mix well. Add tomato, cucumber, and herbs, and season with additional salt if needed. Add a bit of black pepper and drizzle with a tablespoon of olive oil. Mix together and enjoy.

MAIN EVENT DISHES

MAIN EVENT DISHES

3 INGREDIENTS or so…

VEGETABLE BAKE (TIAN)

A tian is a baked dish of artfully arranged vegetable slices. I make it with many veggie variations, depending on what I have on hand at a given moment. The original recipe calls for potatoes, zucchini, and tomatoes, but you could use just the potatoes and zucchini or add a yellow squash or an eggplant instead and skip the tomatoes (although they do add a beautiful red color). If you keep it to any three vegetables, preferably with potatoes as the anchor, it usually comes out looking and tasting very good. Try to choose veggies with about the same diameter to make it easier to arrange the slices.

Serves 4–6

1 large onion, diced

2 garlic cloves, minced

3 tablespoons olive oil, divided

3–4 medium gold potatoes, sliced ¼-inch thick

2 large zucchini or
1 zucchini/1 yellow squash or
1 zucchini/1 eggplant, sliced ¼-inch thick

2–3 medium firm tomatoes (I like plum or Roma tomatoes), sliced ¼-inch thick

Salt and pepper

A pinch of dried thyme or a sprig of fresh thyme

Preheat the oven to 375 degrees F.

Sauté the onions and garlic in 2 tablespoons of olive oil over medium heat until soft and translucent. Spread the mixture on the bottom of a baking dish.

Arrange the veggie slices in tight rows on top of the onion and garlic mixture, alternating the colors. Drizzle with a tablespoon of olive oil. Sprinkle with a pinch of salt, pepper, and thyme.

Cover the dish with unbleached parchment paper *(optional)* and then aluminum foil and bake for 35–40 minutes, until the potatoes are soft.

Remove the foil and parchment paper cover and bake for 5–10 minutes more until the veggies are golden on top. Or sprinkle some grated cheese on top and bake until browned a bit.

ZUCCHINI PASTA WITH BASIL TOMATO SAUCE

If you have a spiralizer, you will have discovered some fun ways to add more veggies to your diet. Here is another one for you. I like this recipe because it makes a warm, real pasta-like dish. Zucchini "noodles" naturally contain plenty of liquid and leaving them to sit for too long might leave you with a zucchini noodle soup instead, so eat them as soon as they are ready!

Serves 4

4 medium zucchini, spiralized into noodles

2 small garlic cloves, minced

2 medium tomatoes, diced (I prefer plum or Roma tomatoes)

¼ cup fresh basil leaves

A pinch of dried thyme *(optional)*

3–4 tablespoons of freshly grated parmesan cheese *(optional)*

3 tablespoons olive oil

Salt and pepper

Add a pinch of salt to the spiralized zucchini, give them a toss and leave them to drain in a colander over a large bowl.

Meanwhile, in a large pan over medium heat, add the olive oil, garlic, and thyme (if using), and sauté for 2–3 minutes. Add the tomatoes and a pinch of salt and pepper, stir gently, and cook for 3-5 more minutes or until the tomatoes are soft and mushy.

Give a good toss to the zucchini to shake off the remaining juices. You can also blot them with a paper towel prior to adding them to the pan with the sauce.

Once in the pan, toss gently to coat the noodles with the sauce and cook for another minute or two. Serve immediately with some fresh basil and a drizzle of olive oil on top, along with some parmesan cheese, if you fancy.

3 INGREDIENTS or so...

ROASTED CHICKEN

I use an oven-safe round baking dish or oval roasting pan deep enough to accommodate the whole chicken and all of the juices that result from the cooking. This recipe requires minimal preparation but yields maximum flavor in the roasted chicken.

Serves 4–6

1 whole organic chicken, giblets removed

2 medium onions (1½ onions diced; ½ onion quartered)

1 small lemon, quartered

Salt and pepper

A sprig of fresh rosemary *(optional)*

1 teaspoon of dried thyme *(optional)*

Preheat the oven to 395 degrees F.

Wash the chicken inside and out and pat dry with paper towels. Generously sprinkle the chicken, including inside the cavity, with salt, pepper, and dried thyme (if using).

Place the lemon and onion quarters inside the chicken; if you have a sprig of fresh rosemary, stuff that inside, too.

Spread the diced onion evenly across the bottom of the baking dish and place the chicken on top. Roast for 1¼ to 1½ hours or until the juices run clear when you cut between the thigh and leg. Remove from the oven, cover with a sheet of unbleached parchment paper with a kitchen towel on top, and let rest for 10–15 minutes. This chicken comes out so juicy—and you will love the bonus "French onion soup" bubbling up on the bottom of the pan!

MEAT PIE

My boys love this pie and it is full of flavor and easy to make. I use organic all-purpose flour and sometimes mix it (50/50) with organic whole-wheat flour for extra texture. When it is right out of the oven, this pie is incredibly juicy, while the crust will break easily and make it difficult to serve in a neat way. Thus, I prefer to let it rest for 10–15 minutes so the juices get reabsorbed a bit and the crust softens too. If your patience permits, let it cool for good 30 minutes before serving. I promise it will taste even better.

Serves 6–8

Dough:

2½ cups of flour (all-purpose or a 50/50 mix of all-purpose and whole-wheat)

8 tablespoons organic grass-fed butter (¼ pound = 4 ounces = 113 g)

¾ cup filtered cold water

A pinch of salt

A pinch of baking soda

Filling:

1 pound grass-fed beef (no particular cut required), cut into ¼-inch cubes

2 medium onions, cut into ¼-inch dice

1 large carrot, cut into ¼-inch dice

1 tablespoon water

Salt and pepper

To make the dough: If your butter is right out of the fridge, cut it into small pieces. This way, it softens quicker. In a large bowl, mix the butter with the flour, a pinch of salt, and a pinch of baking soda. Use a fork or your hands until the dough has the texture of coarse meal. Add the water. Mix it all together and knead it right in the bowl, just enough to bring the dough together.

You may add up to ¼ cup of extra flour if the dough is too sticky. Leave it in the bowl, cover with a kitchen towel, and refrigerate for a minimum of 15 minutes. You can leave the dough overnight if you plan to bake the pie the next day. While the dough is resting in the fridge, make the filling.

Preheat the oven to 375 degrees F.

To make the filling: Using a sharp knife, cut the beef into ¼-inch cubes. (Note: I find it easier to cut meat when it is a little firmed up in the freezer—usually 30 minutes will do the trick.)

Place the meat, onions, and carrots in a large bowl, add 1 tablespoon of water, season with salt and pepper, and mix well. Ideally, use your hands so the mixture blends well and the ingredients begin to release their juices. Set aside.

Remove the dough from the fridge and divide it into two portions, one slightly larger than the other.

Cut parchment paper to fit a large rectangular baking sheet. I use 12.5 x 16-inch parchment paper sheets as they fit perfectly into my baking sheet. Dust the parchment with flour

and roll the larger size dough portion out to almost the same size as the parchment, leaving about an inch of paper open on each side. Place the parchment paper with the dough onto the baking sheet.

Roll the second portion of the dough on a new parchment paper sheet into a slightly smaller rectangle, leaving 2.5–3 inches of paper bordering each side.

Pile the filling onto the larger rectangle and spread it evenly, leaving a 1–1.5-inch dough border on each side. Cover the filling with the second dough rectangle and fold and pinch the edges together to close the pie.

Cut a small opening in the middle of the pie so that steam will escape and the crust will not tear while baking.

Bake for 45–60 minutes or until golden. Remove from the oven and let cool for at least 15 minutes—preferably 30 minutes—before serving.

3 INGREDIENTS or so...

MINI MEATLOAVES

This basic recipe can be used for beef, turkey, or chicken meatloaf. I like to mix organic ground beef with organic ground turkey 50/50 or 60/40 for this recipe. Making it with ground beef or ground chicken alone is equally delicious. This recipe is gluten-, dairy- and egg-free, and includes my little secret for keeping meatloaf juicy and moist: one grated zucchini or yellow squash. I use a large deep baking pan (9 x 13 x 2.5-inch) to keep all the juices in.

Makes 16 mini loaves

2 pounds of organic ground meat—beef, chicken, turkey, or a mix

2 large onions

1 medium to large zucchini or yellow squash, grated

1 tablespoon water

Salt and pepper

Optional ingredients:

½ cup fresh flat-leaf parsley

2 garlic cloves, peeled

1 tablespoon olive oil or avocado oil

Preheat the oven to 400 degrees F.

In a food processor, finely chop the onions, parsley, and optional garlic. Using the large holes of a box grater, grate your zucchini or yellow squash.

Place the ground meat in a large bowl. Add the vegetables, water, salt, and pepper. You may also want to add a tablespoon of olive oil or avocado oil if the ground meat does not have enough fat. Mix it all very well.

Pat the mixture evenly into a large, rectangular baking dish. With your fingers, create a pattern on top of the loaf, dividing it in half lengthwise and into about 8 rectangles widthwise. You will end up marking about 16 same-size rectangles. (See photo.)

Bake uncovered for about 35 minutes until the juices are clear. Remove from the oven, cover with a parchment paper sheet topped with a kitchen towel, and let rest for 10–15 minutes while all the juices get reabsorbed. Cut the rectangles apart and serve with a side of your choice.

PASTA WITH GROUND BEEF, OR NOT YOUR USUAL BOLOGNESE

This is our quick, save-the-dinner dish that my boys absolutely love—and it can be gluten-free if you have gluten-free pasta on hand. Brown rice noodles are great with this dish, while my original recipe calls for organic vegetable radiatore pasta from Trader Joe's. My mom makes it with three ingredients only, while I like to add the tomato, bell pepper, garlic, and parsley for color.

Serves 6–8

1 package organic ground beef (about 1 ⅓ pounds)

1 medium onion, chopped

3–4 tablespoons avocado oil

Salt and pepper

1 package (12–16 ounces) organic pasta of your choice

Optional ingredients:

1 small tomato, diced

½ bell pepper (any color), chopped

1 garlic clove, minced

1/3 cup fresh, flat-leaf parsley, chopped

Bring a pot of water to a boil and cook pasta according to the package instructions.

Meanwhile, set a large pot over medium heat, add the avocado oil and ground meat and sauté, stirring frequently to break up the meat, for about 5 minutes. Add the onion and garlic and sauté for an additional 5–10 minutes until the onions are soft and translucent. Add the tomato and bell pepper and season with salt and black pepper. Sauté for 5 more minutes until the meat is cooked through and the veggies are soft.

Add the cooked pasta, mix it all together, top with the parsley, and voilà: Dinner is ready.

3 INGREDIENTS or so...

DOVER SOLE EN PAPILLOTE

Cooking en papillote is an old-school French technique that means cooking in parchment paper parcels. This recipe is one of my very favorite combinations, but you can experiment with other fish, shellfish, chicken, and many different vegetables. This is an easy and delicious method of cooking, as it keeps all the juices and flavors inside the parcel, the presentation is very appealing, and cleanup is simple!

Serves 4

4 large or 8 small Dover sole fillets, washed and patted dry with paper towels

4 medium golden potatoes, scrubbed

1 celery stalk, julienned

1 carrot, julienned

Olive oil

Salt and pepper

Optional ingredients:

A few fresh, flat parsley leaves

1 teaspoon capers

1 lemon, quartered

Preheat oven to 375 degrees F.

Steam or boil the whole potatoes until almost tender, 7–10 minutes. Meanwhile, cut the other vegetables.

Lay out 4 sheets of parchment paper. Slice the cooked potatoes into ⅓-inch-thick rounds, holding the hot potato with a fork. Lay them down first, in the lower third section of the parchment paper sheet, one whole sliced potato per sheet. Season with salt and drizzle with a bit of olive oil.

Place sole fillets on top of the potato slices, one large or two small per sheet. Divide the celery, carrots, and capers evenly among the four sheets, atop the fillets.

Season with additional salt and pepper and drizzle each with 1½ teaspoons of olive oil. Gently fold the top half of the parchment paper sheet over the fish and bring the edges together to make a rectangle. Fold the edges of the paper to form a sealed parcel. (You may want to use toothpicks or staples for a good seal, but be cautious and use just a few, making sure that they do not get into your food.)

Place the parcels on a baking sheet and bake for 15–25 minutes, depending on the thickness of the fillets. Remove from the oven and let the parcels rest for 5 minutes. Transfer the parcels to plates and serve. When the parcel is opened, you can drizzle with some additional olive oil and a squeeze of fresh lemon.

BROILED SALMON

This is one of the easiest and quickest ways to cook salmon. I use a stoneware baking dish, but you also can use a baking sheet lined with parchment paper.

Serves 4

4 salmon fillets

Ghee or olive oil

Salt and pepper

Preheat the broiler. Place salmon fillets on the baking sheet or in the baking dish. Drizzle each fillet with olive oil or 1–2 teaspoons of ghee, and season with salt and pepper. Broil for 10–15 minutes, depending on how well done you like it.

Remove from oven and drizzle with freshly squeezed lemon juice, if you fancy.

3 INGREDIENTS or so…

WHOLE BAKED SALMON FILLET

I buy a fillet of salmon big enough to fit in my 9 x 13-inch baking dish. One fillet of my favorite wild sockeye salmon usually makes about 6 portions. You can always choose smaller pieces to serve 4 or even 2 people.

Serves 6

Whole salmon fillet

2 sprigs fresh rosemary

2 tablespoons ghee or olive oil

½ lemon, thinly sliced

Salt and pepper

Preheat the oven to 375 degrees F.

Place the salmon fillet in the baking dish, skin down. Drizzle olive oil or scatter ghee evenly on top of the salmon, season generously with salt, and sprinkle with black pepper.

Place the rosemary sprigs and lemon slices evenly on top of the fish. Cover with parchment paper first *(optional)* and then foil, and bake for 15–20 minutes, depending on how well done you like it. Remove from the oven and let rest for at least 5 minutes.

TIP: *Sometimes I like the salmon fillet to get a bit browned on top. After it is cooked, I remove the foil cover, drizzle on a bit of oil, and put the salmon back into the oven to broil for 1–2 minutes, which gives it that golden top right away.*

BAKED BRANZINO
WITH FENNEL, TWO WAYS

You can use any white-meat fish with this easy recipe. However, I love this iconic Mediterranean fish for its delicate flesh and deliciously mild flavor. Branzino (or branzini, in the plural) is sometimes called European sea bass. Most of the time I bake the fish en papillote, making one big parchment paper parcel per fish and placing them on a large baking sheet. Other times, I place both whole branzini in a baking dish and cover it with parchment paper and then foil.

Serves 4

2 whole branzini (ask the fishmonger to clean and gut the fish for you, and to remove the head and tail)

1 fennel bulb, halved and sliced into 1/8-inch half-rounds

Olive oil

Salt and pepper

Preheat the oven to 375 degrees F.

1. Baking en papillote:
Lay out 2 sheets of parchment paper (about 12.5 x 16-inch sheets). Divide the sliced fennel, using half for each sheet. Scatter a few fennel slices on the lower third section of the first parchment sheet and place one whole branzino on top. Drizzle olive oil over the skin and inside of the fish. Season the skin on both sides and on the inside with salt and pepper. Place the remainder of the fennel slices inside the branzino and scattered over the top.

Gently fold the top half of the parchment paper sheet over the fish and bring the edges together to make a rectangle. Fold the edges of the paper to form a sealed parcel. (You may want to use toothpicks or staples for a good seal, but be cautious and use just a few, making sure that they do not get into your food.)

Repeat the steps for the second branzino parcel.

Place the parcels on a baking sheet and bake for 20–30 minutes, depending on the thickness of the fish, until cooked through.* Remove from the oven and let the parcels rest for 5 minutes. Transfer the parcels to plates and serve. When the parcel is opened, you can drizzle with some additional olive oil and a squeeze of fresh lemon.

2. Baking in a dish:

Scatter half of the sliced fennel in a deep baking dish. Drizzle with a bit of olive oil and season with salt. Place the 2 whole, cleaned branzini on top. Drizzle olive oil over the skin and inside of both fish. Season the skin and the inside with salt and pepper. Place the remainder of the fennel slices inside the branzini and scattered over the top.

Cover the baking dish with parchment paper topped with foil and bake for 20–30 minutes, depending on the fish thickness, until cooked through.* Remove from the oven, let rest 5 minutes, and serve hot.

*The fish is cooked though when the flesh is opaque, not translucent, and flakes easily with a fork.

SWEETS

SWEETS

3 INGREDIENTS or so...

SIMPLY DELICIOUS DARK CHOCOLATE

This is my favorite dessert by far! It's not just delicious, it has health-boosting, nutrient-dense ingredients too. Think of it as your superfood dessert! You will not need any fancy equipment or tools to make these decadent-tasting chocolates. Many homemade chocolate recipes use coconut oil, but I prefer to make mine with only cacao butter. They don't melt as fast as with coconut oil, and they really taste and look like those "best in the world" chocolates from the top luxury chocolatier (one caveat, you know the ingredients of your homemade chocolates).

Makes 45–50 chocolates

8 ounces organic cacao powder

8 ounces organic cacao butter

4–5 tablespoons of honey or maple syrup, or use Stevia extract to taste

Optional:
A pinch of salt

Nuts, seeds, or chopped dried fruit

If you do not have chocolate molds, place parchment paper on top of a baking sheet and pour the melted chocolate onto it, creating a big or small chocolate bar. Try not to make it too thick, so it will be easier to break without too much mess. Another idea is to use parchment paper muffin cups as molds, pouring roughly 1–2 tablespoons of the melted chocolate into each one.

Melt cacao butter in a double boiler over medium heat. When fully melted, add cacao powder and stir but do not over-mix. Add honey (or your sweetener of choice).

Taste now for sweetness but be careful, as it could be very hot. Add more sweetener if needed. If you are using any toppings, put them in the molds first before pouring in the chocolate. Once you fill the molds, you can sprinkle a tiny bit of salt on the top (or rather, bottom), of your chocolates.

Leave them in the refrigerator for at least 30 minutes or until completely hardened. Keep them stored in the refrigerator for up to a few weeks.

NUT AND SUPER BERRY CLUSTERS

A delicious combination of dark chocolate and super foods. What could be better?

Makes 20–25 clusters

Use my Simply Delicious Dark Chocolate recipe from page 103, along with dried fruits and nuts mixed and matched in your favorite combination. Chopped dates, dried figs, apricots, mangoes, mulberries, or goji berries are all delicious, as are walnuts, pecans, almonds, hazelnuts, sunflower seeds, and pumpkin seeds.

Use paper muffin cups and put the dried fruit and nuts in a single layer on the bottom, then pour the warm chocolate on top so it holds the nuts and fruits together. I like to then sprinkle just a bit of sea salt on top.

3 INGREDIENTS or so...

PAVLOVA

This is my "prima ballerina" dessert. My kids call it "clouds in heaven," and my friends always ask for it. I used to start making it a day or two in advance, as the egg whites had to sit at room temperature overnight and then the meringue had to dry in the oven for hours. However, I was in Kazakhstan and my sister-in-law, Lenara, made Pavlova that tasted equally delicious without so many lengthy steps. I obviously had to make a few adjustments! It is not sugar-free and it does contain (organic) heavy whipping cream and (pasture-raised) egg whites. But the deliciousness of Pavlova is so worth it. The delicate white meringue with specks of colorful berries will remind you of the white tutu of the famous Russian prima ballerina Anna Pavlova.

Serves 6–8

Meringue:

6 large egg whites

1¼ cups organic fine white sugar

Cream:

16 ounces organic heavy whipping cream

3–4 tablespoons powdered sugar

Topping:

Fresh strawberries, raspberries, and blueberries

A few mint leaves *(optional)*

10 shelled pistachios *(optional)*

Preheat the oven to 300 degrees F.

Place the egg whites in a squeaky clean and dry bowl. Using an electric mixer, beat them on high speed until firm. Continuing on high speed, start gradually adding sugar to the egg whites. Whisk until the meringue makes firm, glossy, and smooth peaks, but do not overdo it.

Line a baking sheet with parchment paper and spread the meringue evenly, forming your desired shape. I make mine round or oval, roughly following the size of my baking sheet but leaving about a one-inch border. Do not worry about a perfectly smooth top; it's actually better to have little peaks and valleys.

Bake the meringue for 1 hour. Turn the oven off, leaving the meringue to rest for another 5–10 minutes in the oven without opening the oven door. The meringue will have a slightly golden color, with a crisp outside and a soft inside. Do not leave the meringue in the oven for too long because it will get too crispy (unless, of course, you prefer it that way).

With an electric mixer, whip the heavy cream with the powdered sugar on high speed until firm. Do not overdo it.

Pile the cream on top of the completely cooled meringue and spread evenly, leaving some small peaks and valleys.

Cut your large strawberries into quarters and scatter all the berries on top of the cream. Add the mint leaves or chopped green pistachios, if desired, et voilà!

TIP: *I make a basic pastry with the leftover yolks. See the recipe on page 110. Note that you will have to double the quantity of each ingredient in the recipe as written if you want to use all the yolks. You can refrigerate this pastry dough for up to 3 days or freeze it for up to a month.*

HONEY APPLE TART

I absolutely love this easy dessert and it is my saving grace when I have yolks left over from the Pavlova recipe! I usually make the basic pastry dough in advance and store it in the freezer. Then when I want to make dessert, I remove the pastry from the freezer about an hour before I need to use it. After that, this tart can be assembled in no time and popped into the oven. I have made it with many different fruits but I find it works best with apples, pears, or peaches.

Serves 6–8

Pastry:

8 tablespoons organic grass-fed butter (¼ pound = 4 ounces = 113 g)

1½ cups organic all-purpose flour

3 egg yolks

1 teaspoon sugar

A pinch of salt

5 tablespoons water

Filling:

3–4 large apples, peeled, cored, and sliced ¼-inch thick

1 tablespoon brown sugar *(optional)*

1 tablespoon butter, cut into small bits

3–4 tablespoons raw honey

For the pastry, beat the soft butter with the sugar and salt; I use either a fork or a wooden spoon. Add the egg yolks, water, and flour. Bring it all together, kneading just a little to form a smooth ball. If the pastry is too crumbly you may add a tablespoon of water, or if it is too sticky add a tablespoon of flour. Wrap the dough in plastic and refrigerate for at least 1 hour.

Preheat the oven to 375 degrees F.

Prepare the apples. Remove the pastry from the refrigerator, let it rest at room temperature for 10–15 minutes, then roll onto a single layer of parchment paper to about the same size as your baking sheet or slightly smaller. Arrange the apple slices in rows slightly overlapping each other. Cover the entire surface with apples. Sprinkle with a tablespoon of brown sugar (if using) and the bits of butter.

Bake for 30–40 minutes or until the pastry and apples are slightly browned. Remove from the oven and let cool for 5 minutes. Drizzle generously with honey, so it evenly covers the warm apple tart with extra sweetness. Serve warm or cold.

3 INGREDIENTS or so...

TAHINI CHOCOLATE PASTE

I love tahini! These ground sesame seeds are rich in essential nutrients, vitamins, minerals, and healthy fat. Most recipes use tahini in savory dishes and sauces; however, it can work really well in desserts, too. This particular recipe was inspired by Katy Allan, a food blogger I started following recently. I just loved her presentation, and sticking to my favorite healthy ingredients produced this yummy goodness.

Makes 1 generous portion

2 tablespoons tahini

1 tablespoon cacao powder

1 teaspoon honey

½ cup of fresh organic berries and/or pomegranate arils (seeds)

In a small bowl mix tahini, cacao powder, and honey. Top with berries and enjoy. If the paste is too dry for you, mix in a teaspoon or two of olive oil.

OATMEAL COOKIES

Oatmeal cookies are such a treat, especially when they're made with the wholesome ingredients in this recipe. These are also gluten-, dairy-, and egg-free.

Makes 15–18 cookies

1 cup organic, gluten-free rolled oats

½ cup almond flour or other gluten-free flour

3 tablespoons coconut oil

⅓ cup maple syrup or organic sugar or 4 drops of stevia

1 tablespoon chia seeds, soaked in 4 tablespoons of water for 10–15 minutes

1 ripe/spotty banana, mashed

A pinch of baking soda

A pinch of salt

Preheat the oven to 350 degrees F.

Mash the banana in a bowl. Add soaked chia seeds, coconut oil, and maple syrup to the banana and mix it all together. Add a pinch of salt and a pinch of soda to the mash. Add the almond flour, give it another mix, and then incorporate the oats into the mixture until well combined. Chill the dough in the refrigerator for about 15 minutes.

Line a baking sheet with parchment paper. With a table-spoon, scoop balls of dough onto the baking sheet, making 15–18 cookies. Bake for 10–15 minutes, until golden on top. Remove from the oven and let cool for 5 minutes, then transfer to a wooden board or wire rack to cool completely.

3 INGREDIENTS or so...

COCONUT MATCHA (OR CHOCOLATE) ICE CREAM

This dairy-free ice cream is best when served fresh; however, you can freeze it for up to two weeks. Make chocolate ice cream by substituting cacao powder for the matcha powder.

Serves 4

2 cans (13.5 ounces each) organic coconut cream

1½ tablespoons matcha powder (or cacao powder)

4 tablespoons maple syrup

1 teaspoon rum or vodka *(optional)*

Seeds from 1 vanilla pod *(optional)*

Place all the ingredients into a blender and blend on high speed for one or two minutes until the mixture is creamy and smooth. Transfer into a pre-chilled ice-cream maker and churn according to the manufacturer's instructions.

Once ready, serve the soft ice cream immediately. You can top it with chopped pistachios, walnuts, coconut flakes, cacao nibs, pomegranate seeds, or whatever toppings you fancy.

DRINKS

DRINKS

There are times when nothing gives that pick-me-up effect like a cup of warm tea or a glass of freshly squeezed juice. Generally liquids require little time to digest and absorb, thus you feel their effects fairly quickly.

ACCIDENTAL MATCHA

I had tried matcha drinks elsewhere many times and I wasn't sure if it was a drink for me. Matcha powder is finely ground green tea leaves. While green tea is packed with antioxidants, anti-inflammatory agents, vitamins, and minerals, matcha powder is even more potent, with a greater concentration of green tea's beneficial components. One day, I decided to try making a matcha drink at home, given that I had some leftover matcha powder (from a failed attempt at making green chocolate) along with some collagen powder (great for skin, hair, and nails), which I was eager to use more often. So here is what came out. To me, it tastes really good.

Makes 1 cup

6–8 cashews, soaked in hot water for at least 3 minutes

½ teaspoon matcha powder

1 cup hot water

1 tablespoon collagen powder *(optional)*

Rinse the cashew nuts and combine all the ingredients in a high-speed blender. Blend for 30–60 seconds and enjoy.

I like to experiment with different ingredients for my matcha. Sometimes I use a tablespoon of hemp seeds instead of cashew nuts. I like adding a teaspoon of MCT oil (a fat usually extracted from coconut oil) for sharper brain, energy, and a little extra froth. Or I add ¼ teaspoon of maca powder (a plant-based superfood native to Peru) for extra nutrition, hormonal balance and stamina. I always suggest keeping it simple, though, and not overdoing the number of ingredients.

RED DETOX JUICE

There are numerous versions of fresh juices. Here is the juice that my parents used to make, from as long ago as I can remember. I've made just a few modifications, but it still tastes great and is very refreshing and detoxifying too.

Serves 1

1 medium beet

2 carrots

6 celery stalks

½ lemon

Wash all the ingredients. I usually peel only the beet. I don't mind the skin and the seeds from the lemon and they contain as much vitamin C as the whole lemon itself. Beets are incredibly good for blood detoxification and are an excellent source of iron, while the vitamin C from the lemon is important for iron absorption. Cut the ingredients to fit in your juicer. Juice all the ingredients and enjoy right away.

GREEN JUICE

Everyone knows about the super powers of green juice. There are dozens of variations of green ingredients, but here is my basic formula.

Serves 1

8 celery stalks

1 green apple

1 inch of ginger

⅓ lemon

1 small cucumber *(optional)*

Wash and cut all the ingredients to fit in the juicer. I leave the lemon and apple skin and seeds intact (remove the stem) and I rarely peel the ginger. Juice all the ingredients and enjoy right away.

IMMUNE-BOOSTING TEA

This is my favorite tea during the colder months, but you can also drink it cold, so it is very refreshing in the summer too. When you are feeling under the weather, this tea will give your immune system an instant boost. Sometimes I like to drink it with a teaspoon of raw honey.

Serves 1

⅔-inch piece fresh ginger, washed and thinly sliced

½-inch piece fresh turmeric, washed and thinly sliced

½ lemon, washed and thinly sliced

½ orange, washed and thinly sliced

3–4 cups of hot water

Although I try to stick to organic options for these ingredients, it is important to wash them really well and leave the skins intact. Thinly slice all the ingredients, put them in a teapot, and cover with hot water. Close the lid and cover with a tea cozy or kitchen towel to keep the tea warm. Let it steep for 15–30 minutes. The longer it steeps, the richer the taste.

EASY BASICS

EASY BASICS

3 INGREDIENTS or so...

THE BASICS OF HOW AND WHY TO SOAK NUTS

Nuts and seeds can be powerhouse ingredients in your diet. They are rich in healthy fat, protein, vitamins, minerals, and fiber. However, while nuts and seeds are extremely nutritious and the modern world provides us with readily available shelled varieties, they are also rather easy to overeat. Hence, I need to remind you about moderation when it comes to consuming them. A handful or two a day is plenty to enjoy all of their benefits.

One more important trick when it comes to consuming nuts and seeds is to soak them first. Soaking activates beneficial enzymes, making the nuts easier to digest and their nutrients easier to absorb. The soaking process germinates nuts and neutralizes anti-nutrients and enzyme inhibitors like lectins and phytates. It also enhances the flavor of the nuts, while increasing the nutritional potency of vitamins A, C, and B, and proteins.

1 cup raw nuts

2 cups of room-temperature or warm filtered water

A pinch of salt *(optional)*

Soaking Times

Almonds: 8–12 hours

Brazil nuts: 4 hours

Cashews: 2–4 hours

Hazelnuts: 8–12 hours

Pecans: 4 hours

Walnuts: 4 hours

Pumpkin seeds: 8 hours

Sesame seeds: 8 hours

Sunflower seeds: 2 hours

Place the nuts in a glass bowl and cover with filtered water. You should use a ratio of at least twice the amount of water to nuts so that they are covered by an inch or two. Add a pinch of sea salt or Himalayan pink salt if you like. Leave the nuts overnight or check the table on the left for the ideal soaking times for different nuts and seeds.

After the nuts are soaked, drain off the soaking water as it will contain all the anti-nutrients. Then rinse the nuts well until the water runs clear. Dry very well with paper towels, or spread them on a parchment-covered baking sheet and dry them in your oven at lowest possible setting, 120–150 degrees F. You may also use a dehydrator according to the dehydrator's instructions. Be sure they are completely dry before storing, as they can quickly gather unwanted mold.

I usually soak a cup or two at a time, dry them thoroughly with paper towels, and then spread them evenly on a dry paper towel on the countertop for a few hours or the whole day. Make sure they are not in high-humidity area, as they will not dry at all.

HOMEMADE NUT MILKS

There is nothing better than homemade nut milk. Making your own means no additives, no preservatives, and complete control over the quality of what goes in and what comes out—the flavors, the textures, everything! Just be sure to read through the recipes first, as you will need to build in time for soaking the nuts.

You will need a good, high-speed blender. I like using my Vitamix. Most of the milks require only two ingredients: nuts and water. However, you can experiment and add dates or maple syrup for extra sweetness; a few tablespoons of cacao powder for a chocolate flavor; cinnamon or/and turmeric to spice it up; or a pinch of sea salt.

Try different combinations and see what you like best. I prefer to stick to the basic two.

CASHEW MILK

With a high-speed blender, it will take you no time to make this delicious dairy-free milk. Cashews are naturally sweet and the milk comes out creamy and rich, with no need for straining. If you want more sweetness, add one or two pitted dates, or a teaspoon of maple syrup. You can add a pinch of sea salt too.

Makes 3 cups of milk

1 cup raw, organic cashews

2 cups filtered water, for soaking

3 cups filtered water, for blending with the nuts

Soak 1 cup of cashews in 2 cups of water for at least 2 hours or up to 4 hours. (In a pinch, soak for 10 minutes in hot water.) Rinse them well so the water runs clear.

Place the soaked nuts in a high-speed blender with 3 cups of water and blend on high for 1–2 minutes. Pour and enjoy! Store the cashew milk in an airtight glass container for up to 3 days in the refrigerator.

HEMP MILK

Hemp seeds are a great source of a complete protein, containing all the amino acids. Not only that, they contain calcium, magnesium, iron, B vitamins, fiber, and potassium as well.

Hemp milk is the easiest of all to make! It does not require soaking or straining. However, if you prefer a smoother consistency or want to use it in a recipe that calls for a smoother consistency, you can use a nut milk bag, cheesecloth, or even a knee-high sheer nylon hosiery to strain the milk.

Makes 3 cups of milk

1 cup raw, shelled hemp seeds

3 cups filtered water

*Optional ingredients
(use one or any combination):*

2–4 pitted dates

1–2 tablespoons maple syrup

1–2 tablespoons cacao powder

A pinch of salt

Place the hemp seeds and water in a high-speed blender. Blend on high for one minute or until the seeds are completely pulverized. You can enjoy the hemp milk right away or strain it through a nut-milk bag, cheesecloth, or knee-high sheer nylon hosiery for a smoother consistency.

Note: If you are adding a sweetener or optional flavoring, I suggest adding it after you strain the milk. Return the strained milk to the blender, add the flavoring, and blend on high for another minute or so until smooth and creamy.

Store hemp milk in an airtight glass container for up to 3 days in the refrigerator.

ALMOND MILK

One of the most popular dairy-free milks is almond milk. Making it yourself is the best way to guarantee the quality of the nuts and the absence of additives and preservatives. Almond milk has a very mild flavor and a rich and creamy consistency. I prefer to make mine with just two ingredients: almonds and water. However, you can add flavor with dates, pure maple syrup, a pinch of sea salt, cacao powder, cinnamon, or turmeric.

Makes 3 cups of milk

1 cup raw, organic almonds

2 cups filtered water, for soaking

3 cups filtered water, for blending with the nuts

*Optional ingredients
(use one or any combination):*

2–4 pitted dates

1–2 tablespoons maple syrup

1–2 tablespoons cacao powder

A pinch of cinnamon

A pinch of turmeric

A pinch of salt

Soak 1 cup of almonds in 2 cups of filtered water at room temperature overnight (8–12 hours). Drain off the soaking water and rinse the almonds well so the water runs clear.

Place the rinsed almonds in the blender with 3 cups of water and blend at high speed for about one minute, until nuts are completely pulverized. You can enjoy the almond milk at this stage, with "pulp," or if you prefer a smoother consistency, strain it using a nut milk bag, cheesecloth, or knee-high sheer nylon hosiery.

Note: If you are using an optional flavoring, I suggest adding it after you strain the milk. Return the strained milk to the blender, add the flavoring, and blend on high for another minute or so until smooth and creamy.

Store almond milk in an airtight glass container for up to 3 days in the refrigerator.

3 INGREDIENTS or so...

SAUERKRAUT (FERMENTED CABBAGE)

There is growing awareness about the powerful health benefits of fermented vegetables. Fermentation increases the bioavailability of the nutrients, while "good" bacteria can improve digestion and build a stronger immune system, just to give a few examples.

Here is my take on a recipe that a friend of mine, Oxana Zubkova, shared with me years ago. Please note that my sauerkraut comes out slightly different every time. Don't give up if your kraut doesn't taste as expected the first time you try this recipe. It will most likely taste different the next time—even when you follow all of the same measurements and directions. The way I like to explain this is that it is simply a live product and it changes! I use a tall glass jar with an airtight lid.

1 large head green cabbage, shredded

1–3 medium carrots, julienned *(optional)*

Mix the shredded cabbage and carrots (if using) in a bowl. I like to add carrots to my sauerkraut for their bright color and additional health benefits. Carrots are also naturally sweet and facilitate the fermentation process.

Stuff your cabbage and carrots into the glass container; pack it tightly, leaving just an inch or so on top. Add filtered water to cover the cabbage completely and close the lid tightly.

Place the jar on a plate or in a bowl, as some water will manage to escape. Leave it on the countertop for a minimum of 48 hours. Do not be alarmed by the bubbling sounds your cabbage will be making—it's a normal part of the process!

I usually open the lid within 48–72 hours and then let the cabbage "burp." Be prepared for a really smelly burp. I like to take it outside before I open the lid, and then cover with a cheesecloth and let it air out for good 30 minutes. Set an alarm so you don't accidentally leave it outside for much longer than that. Store your fermented cabbage in the refrigerator for up to a few weeks.

Add a bit of olive oil and salt before serving your cabbage and enjoy. Or try the salad recipe on page 69.

You also may try fermenting red cabbage, which yields sauerkraut with a beautiful deep purple color. Follow the same process as with green cabbage.

FEEL-BETTER BROTH
(BASIC CHICKEN BROTH)

I think every culture has its own version of a broth with healing properties. If I start to feel under the weather, I immediately make this chicken broth. Sipping it on its own gives comfort and that feel-better effect right away. Cooking the chicken for at least one hour will suffice for basic chicken broth.

Makes 6–8 cups

1 whole organic chicken, giblets removed

1 large carrot, cut to fit in your stockpot

1 medium yellow onion, peeled

2 celery stalks

2 garlic cloves (optional)

5–6 whole black peppercorns *(optional)*

Salt and pepper

Put the chicken in a large stockpot and cover completely with cold water. Bring to a boil, then remove from heat, carefully discard the water, and rinse the chicken.

Return the chicken to the stockpot and again add water to cover it completely. Bring to a boil, then add onions, carrots, celery, garlic, and peppercorns. Make sure the chicken remains fully submerged. Return to a boil, reduce the heat to medium low, add 1½ teaspoons of salt, and let simmer for 1 hour with the lid slightly open.

Remove the chicken and veggies and strain the broth through a fine colander. Add extra salt and pepper, if desired, and it is ready to be sipped on its own. Or, use the broth and the chicken meat as a base for any soup recipe.

TIP 1: *For a richer chicken bone broth, remove the chicken after you simmer it for 1 hour, pick off the meat, and return the bones and carcass to the stock. Simmer for 4–6 hours. Make sure you have enough liquid that the chicken is fully submerged at all times.*

TIP 2: *A money-saving alternative is to use a half-chicken or just two whole chicken legs, instead of a whole chicken, to make the broth. Keep the rest of the ingredients the same and be sure you have enough water to keep all ingredients completely submerged (approximately 8 cups).*

BASIC VEGETABLE STOCK

It is easy to make this nutritious stock that can be used as a base for soups and sauces, or even sipped like tea. The only trick is to avoid starchy vegetables, as they will make your stock cloudy. Onions, garlic, carrots, leeks, fennel, celery, and parsnips add lots of flavor and nutrients to this stock. If you like a meaty flavor, try adding mushrooms. There is no need to chop your veggies, except to make them fit into the stockpot. You can use any combination of veggies depending on what you like and have on hand. Here is a basic recipe.

Makes 6–8 cups

2 whole onions, peeled

2 large carrots, cut to fit in the stockpot

2–4 celery stalks, cut to fit in the stockpot

1 fennel bulb

3 garlic cloves, peeled or unpeeled

1 bunch parsley

Put all the vegetables in the large stockpot, fully cover with water and bring to a boil. Reduce heat to medium low and simmer for 45–60 minutes. Check occasionally to be sure all the veggies are fully submerged; add water if necessary.

Remove from the heat. After it cools, strain through a fine-mesh sieve. Add salt and pepper to taste and enjoy as is or use as a base for soups or sauces.

TIP: *It is a good idea to prepare vegetable stock when you have some free time, and then keep it in the freezer for later use. It is also very good as a substitute for plain water when cooking grains, as it adds extra nutrients and flavor.*

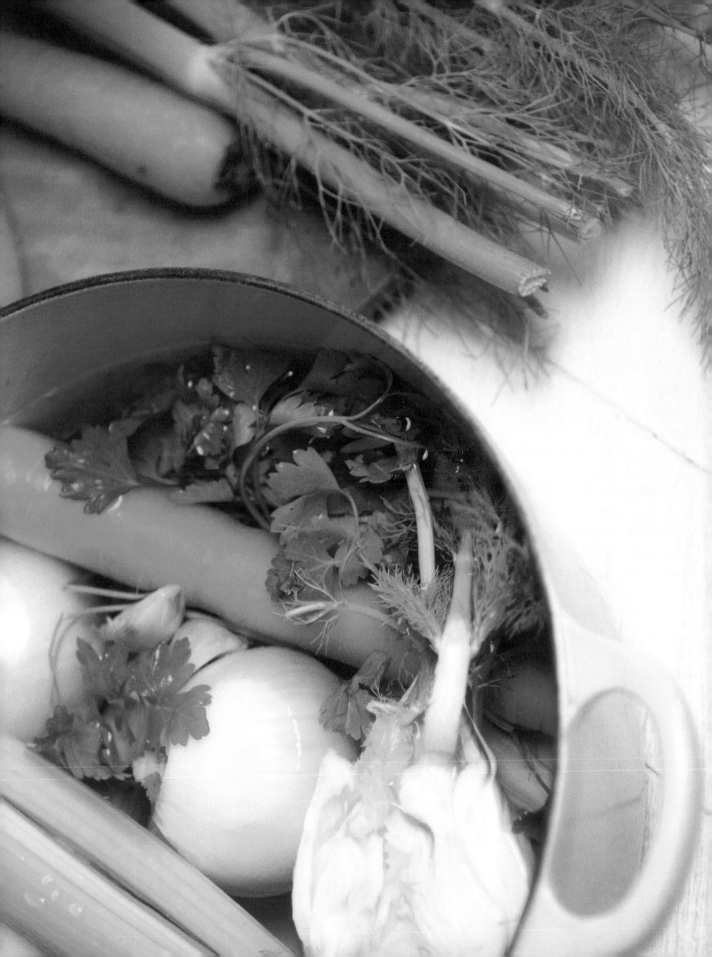

THE BASICS OF COOKING GRAINS

Grains are a great source of vitamins, minerals, fiber, and protein. They are very versatile, working in sweet or savory, cold or hot dishes. They make a great side dish or can be mixed into a salad, soup, or stew, adding extra texture and goodness to any dish.

When I have time, I pre-soak grains for a minimum of an hour or even overnight. The soaking makes grains more digestible and washes away most of the phytic acid that interferes with mineral absorption. Note that pre-soaked grains will cook much faster and require less water. However, if you do not have that extra hour, go ahead and cook your grains anyway. Adding high-quality sea salt or a thumb-sized piece of kombu seaweed will help to infuse the grains with extra minerals and neutralize the acid-forming properties, too—just be sure to discard the kombu before eating.

Cooking grains in vegetable stock instead of water will also infuse them with extra nutrients. For most grains, the cooking proportion is 1 cup of grains to 2 cups of liquid.

Finally, I sometimes add a teaspoon or so of grass-fed butter to cooked grains, as it brings up the flavors and enhances the nutritional content too, adding omega-3s and vitamins.

In the following pages are the instructions for cooking some of my favorite grains. Each grain is different and has its own nutritional profile and benefits. (See pages 15–16 for more information.)

BUCKWHEAT

Makes about 2 cups

1 cup buckwheat

2 cups water

A pinch of salt

Place buckwheat in a fine-mesh strainer and rinse until the water runs clear. Place the rinsed buckwheat into a saucepan with 2 cups of water and bring to a boil. Add a pinch of salt. Let the buckwheat boil for 1 minute, reduce the heat, and simmer for 10–15 minutes, covered but with the lid slightly open, until the water is completely absorbed and the buckwheat is on the soft side but not soggy. Turn off the heat and let it rest, covered, for 5–10 minutes before serving.

MILLET

Makes about 2 cups

1 cup millet

2 cups water

A pinch of salt

Place 1 cup of millet in a bowl, cover it completely with water and let it sit for a minute or two, then rinse well through a fine-mesh strainer so the water runs clear. Place the rinsed millet into a saucepan, cover with 2 cups of water, and bring to a boil. Add a pinch of salt, let it boil for 1 minute, then reduce the heat and simmer for 10–15 minutes, covered but with the lid slightly open, until the water is completely absorbed and the millet looks fluffy and not mushy. Turn off the heat and let the millet rest, covered, for at least 5 minutes. Fluff with a fork and serve.

Buckwheat

Millet

3 INGREDIENTS or so...

QUINOA

Makes about 1¾ cups

1 cup quinoa

1¾ cups water

A pinch of salt

Rinse quinoa in a fine-mesh strainer until the water runs clear. Place quinoa into a saucepan and cover with 1¾ cups of water. Bring it to a boil, add a pinch of salt, and let it boil for 1 minute. Reduce the heat, cover, and let simmer for 10–15 minutes until the water is fully absorbed and the quinoa looks fluffy but not mushy. Turn off the heat and let the quinoa rest, covered, for at least 5 minutes. Fluff with a fork and serve.

ROLLED OATS

Makes about 2 cups

1 cup oats

2 cups water

A pinch of salt

1 teaspoon grass-fed butter *(optional)*

Place the oats in a saucepan, add the water, and bring to a boil. Add a pinch of salt and let boil for 1 minute. Reduce the heat, cover, and let simmer for 5–7 minutes, stirring occasionally. Turn off the heat, keep covered, and let the oats rest for a few minutes before serving. Add the butter, if desired.

Quinoa

Rolled Oats

OLIVE OIL & LEMON DRESSING

My favorite dressing also happens to be the easiest one.
Its clean, crisp, spring taste goes well with pretty much any salad.

Makes enough for a 5-ounce box of greens/4 side salads

Whisk the ingredients together in a small bowl or measuring cup and voilà! You can easily make more or less of this dressing and vary the proportions according to your taste.

4 tablespoons olive oil

1 tablespoon lemon juice

Salt and pepper

OLIVE OIL & BALSAMIC VINEGAR DRESSING

I especially like this dressing with tomatoes and basil.

Makes enough for a 5-ounce box of greens/4 side salads

Whisk all the ingredients together in a small bowl or a measuring cup.

4 tablespoons olive oil

2 teaspoons balsamic vinegar

A pinch of salt

CLASSIC VINAIGRETTE

Makes enough for a 5-ounce box of greens/4 side salads

Whisk all the ingredients in a small bowl or a measuring cup until the dressing is emulsified.

4 tablespoons olive oil

¼ teaspoon Dijon mustard

¼ teaspoon minced garlic *(optional)*

1 teaspoon white wine vinegar or apple cider vinegar

Salt and pepper

INDEX

ABOUT THE AUTHOR

Highly sought-after wellness expert Tamila Urazayeva is a certified integrative nutrition health coach, author, and speaker. She is known for her focus on quality when it comes to food choices, and her talent for showing how integrating small, easy, yet very effective changes into our daily lives can help us achieve maximum wellness.

Having lived in several different countries during the course of her career in international finance, Tamila brings an uncommonly broad perspective on nutrition, health, and wellness to her work.

ACKNOWLEDGMENTS

Special thanks to all my family and friends, my clients, and my book publishing team who supported me throughout the making of this book. Your encouragement and feedback made this book possible the way it is. This list includes but is not limited to:

Mom, Dad, Sergey, Daniel, and Andrew

Poopak Mahdavi, Amie Olson, Alison Hall, Judy Gordon
Your talents and hard work helped realize my vision

Dr. Dana Neacsu, MD

Katya Thornton

Eleonora Batalova

Irina Khomenko

Lenara Batalova

Carol Grunert

IIN Launch Your Dream Book Course team

CPSIA information can be obtained
at www.ICGtesting.com
Printed in the USA
LVHW072303120319
610459LV00008B/38/P